TAILGATES

to

TOUCHDOWNS

fabulous football food

TAILGATES to TOUCHDOWNS
fabulous football food

Willing Vessel Books
Cedar Rapids, Iowa
www.tailgatestotouchdowns.com

nina swan-kohler

Library of Congress Control Number: 2003101808
Swan-Kohler, Nina

ISBN 0-9727760-0-1
First printing, 2003
Printed in Cedar Rapids, Iowa.

Recipe development and testing: Nina Swan-Kohler
Recipe assistance: Linda Behrends and Tami Leonard
Kitchen assistance: Lorrianne Dunn
Chief recipe taste-tester: Ronald Kohler
Photo art direction: Carol Sears and Nina Swan-Kohler
Food and prop styling: Nina Swan-Kohler
Food styling assistance: Tami Leonard
Photographers: John Thomas, Brook Lightner and Steve Herder
Recipe coordination: Susan Carroll
Recipe and copy editing: Donna Lunstrum
Indexing: Donna Lunstrum
Cookbook design and layout: Amanda Smith

Featured Food Products:
C. H. Guenther & Son, Inc. – Pioneer Brand
Pioneer Brand Buttermilk Biscuit & Baking Mix, Pioneer Brand
Gravy Mixes (Brown, Country, Peppered)
C. H. Guenther & Son, Inc. – The White Lily Foods Company
White Lily All-Purpose Flour, White Lily Self-Rising Flour,
White Lily Self-Rising Cornmeal Mix, White Lily Banana Nut Muffin Mix
T. W. Burleson & Sons – Burleson's Pure Clover Honey
Burleson's Pure Clover Honey

PUBLISHER
Willing Vessel Books
d/b/a Swan-Kohler & Associates
P.O. Box 11151
Cedar Rapids, Iowa 52410
www.tailgatestotouchdowns.com

I dedicate this cookbook to my dad,
the first person in my life to demonstrate
a fanatical love of both football and food.

ACKNOWLEDGEMENTS

A hearty "thank you" to all those who encouraged me to write a cookbook or who assisted in the production of this book; so many people deserve thanks. Susan Carroll helped compile my collection of recipes, developed through the years, into one organized file. Donna Lunstrum provided invaluable copy editing skills, but, more importantly, ongoing professional support and encouragement. Amanda Smith did an amazing job with the graphic design. Throughout the entire process, she persevered to perfect all the details. And, my favorite photographer, John Thomas, went beyond my expectations with his talent for making my foods look especially good.

Thank you to Robert Schupbach from Pioneer, Tripp Holmgrain and Belinda Ellis from White Lily, and Jim Phillips from Burleson's for their partnership and support, and for providing their delicious products for recipe development and testing.

I especially want to thank my husband, Ronald, who never ceases to encourage and support me in my various projects. He's my best taste-tester, too!

Without the support of my family, especially my mother, and my circle of personal and professional friends, this book would not have come together. *Thanks to you all!*

12

KICK-OFF

introduction

15

TAILGATES

pre-game munchies

27

THE GRIDIRON

grilled to perfection

39

SIDELINES

sauces, salsas + spreads

TAILGATES

pre-game munchies

Whichever team you support, you're sure to score big when you serve flavor-filled "football food." It's both fashionable and fun to serve food outside, either at pre-game parties at home or at a tailgate party from the back of your vehicle outside the football stadium.

Instead of serving the same old chips and store-bought dip, impress your fellow football fans with hearty and flavorful homemade appetizers for your next tailgate party. Tailgate snacks and meals need to be simple to transport. If you've made the recipe ahead of time, reheat it just before you leave for the game.

TAILGATER'S TEX-MEX CHILI DIP

Cumin adds a kick to this flavorful dip.

1 lb. lean ground pork or beef
2 cups chunky salsa (mild, medium or hot)
1 cup water (divided)
1 package (1.61 oz.) brown gravy mix
  (Pioneer Brand recommended)

½ teaspoon ground cumin
1 can (15 oz.) black beans, rinsed and drained
1 to 2 teaspoons finely chopped jalapeño pepper
  (optional)
Tortilla chips or crackers

In 2-quart saucepan or large skillet, cook and stir ground pork until pork is no longer pink; drain. Add salsa and ½ cup water; heat to boiling. Meanwhile, dissolve gravy mix in ½ cup cool water; stir in cumin. Stir into boiling mixture; cook and stir until thickened. Stir in beans and jalapeño pepper. Reduce heat and simmer 10 minutes. Garnish with fresh cilantro leaves, if desired. Serve with tortilla chips. Makes 10 to 12 servings.

Chili Dip Quesadillas: Spread dip on flour tortillas; sprinkle with shredded cheese. Place another flour tortilla over each. Cook on hot griddle for 2 to 3 minutes per side. Cut into quarters.

extra point

You can make this dip a couple of days ahead of game day; just reheat it in the microwave before serving.

GAME DAY HEARTY MEXICAN DIP

This chunky, cheesy dip makes enough for a crowd. Invite the gang over to watch the game.

1 lb. lean ground beef

1 medium onion, finely chopped (1 cup)

1¾ cups mild picante sauce or 1 can (14½ oz.) Mexican-style diced tomatoes

1 can (4 oz.) chopped green chilies

1 cup water (divided)

1 package (2.75 oz.) country gravy mix (regular or no fat; Pioneer Brand recommended)

8 oz. Mexican-flavored pasteurized prepared cheese product, cubed (Velveeta recommended)

1 teaspoon ground cumin

1 teaspoon finely chopped jalapeño pepper (optional)

Chunks of French bread, tortilla chips or corn chips

In 4-quart saucepan or Dutch oven, cook and stir ground beef and onion until beef is browned; drain. Add picante sauce, green chilies and ½ cup water; heat to boiling. Meanwhile, dissolve gravy mix in ½ cup cool water; stir into boiling mixture until slightly thickened. Reduce heat to low; stir in cheese until melted. Stir in cumin and jalapeño pepper. Heat through. Serve warm with bread chunks, tortilla chips or corn chips. Makes 4 cups.

extra point ● *Substitute regular shredded pasteurized prepared cheese product for the Mexican-flavored cheese; increase cumin to 1½ teaspoons.*

PRE-GAME PINWHEELS

The fresh basil makes these pinwheel biscuits extra tasty.

3 cups buttermilk biscuit & baking mix
   (Pioneer Brand recommended)
3 tablespoons chopped fresh basil leaves
   (or 1½ teaspoons dried basil leaves)
1 cup skim milk

3 tablespoons bottled Caesar salad dressing
¾ cup freshly grated Parmesan cheese or finely
   shredded mozzarella cheese
Garlic salt
½ jar (28-oz. size) hearty tomato spaghetti sauce

In large bowl, stir together biscuit and baking mix, basil and milk to form a stiff dough. If biscuit dough is sticky, add additional biscuit and baking mix as needed to form stiff dough. Turn out onto surface dusted with additional biscuit and baking mix; knead 10 times. Roll out dough into a 12x9-inch rectangle about ¼-inch thick. Spread with salad dressing; sprinkle with cheese. Beginning with long side, roll up one half of dough toward the center (like a jelly roll). Roll other half toward center. Cut down the center to make 2 rolls. Cut each roll into 12 slices; place slices on baking sheet coated with cooking spray. Sprinkle slices with garlic salt. Bake at 400° for 12 to 14 minutes or until pinwheels are golden brown. Meanwhile, heat spaghetti sauce until hot. Serve warm pinwheels with spaghetti sauce. Makes 24 pinwheels.

extra point ❧ *To quickly and easily cut slices of biscuit dough, simply wrap a piece of clean dental floss around the dough. Cross over and pull in opposite directions.*

CHEESY PIGS IN BLANKETS

These "pigskin" classics are delicious dipped in catsup, mustard, barbecue sauce or salsa.

Blankets:
$2/3$ cup shortening
2 $1/4$ cups low-protein self-rising flour
   (White Lily Brand recommended)
1 cup self-rising cornmeal mix
   (White Lily Brand recommended)

1 $1/4$ cups buttermilk
1 cup shredded Cheddar cheese (4 oz.)
Pigs:
1 package (1 lb.) mini smoked sausages (about 48)

In large bowl, using a pastry blender or two knives, cut shortening into flour and cornmeal mix until shortening pieces are the size of small peas. Stir in buttermilk and cheese until dough forms a ball. Turn dough out onto surface dusted with additional flour. Fold dough in half 5 to 7 times to knead (do not overwork dough), adding just enough flour to keep dough from sticking to your hands. Divide dough into 6 balls. Gently roll out each ball to $1/4$-inch thickness (about a 6-inch circle). Using a pizza cutter, cut each circle into 8 wedges. Place smoked sausage on rounded side of each wedge. Roll dough around sausage toward center. Place on baking sheet coated with cooking spray. Bake at 500° for 8 to 10 minutes or until golden brown. Makes 48 appetizers.

extra point ● *If you plan to cook burgers or brats on the grill, simply wrap these appetizers (already baked) in foil and heat them on the grill while the coals are heating.*

FOOTBALL PORK POCKETS

Chipotle chili pepper seasons these pork—filled biscuits for a delicious flavor combination.

¼ cup (½ stick) firm butter or margarine

4 cups buttermilk biscuit & baking mix
 (Pioneer Brand recommended)

½ teaspoon garlic powder

1 cup milk

2 cups shredded Monterey Jack or Cheddar
 cheese (divided)

3 or 4 boneless pork chops (about 1 lb.), cut into
 small cubes

1⅓ cups prepared chipotle chili-style salsa or
 other salsa (divided)

In large bowl, using a pastry blender or two knives, cut butter into biscuit and baking mix and garlic powder to form coarse crumbs. Stir in milk and 1 cup of the cheese to form stiff dough. Turn out onto surface dusted with additional biscuit and baking mix; knead 10 to 12 times. Cover; let rest 5 minutes. Meanwhile, in nonstick skillet over medium-high heat, cook and stir pork cubes until cooked through and no longer pink. Add ⅔ cup of the salsa; stir to combine. Remove from heat and set aside. Divide dough in half. Roll out one half to ¼-inch thickness. Using a 3-inch football-shaped cookie cutter, cut into 16 biscuits. Place on baking sheet coated with cooking spray. Spoon pork mixture onto biscuits, placing 3 or 4 pork cubes on the center of each biscuit. Sprinkle each with cheese. Set aside. Roll out and cut remaining dough as directed above. Place biscuits over cheese and pork mixture; pinch edges together to seal. Prick tops several times with fork to resemble laces on football. Bake at 375° for 15 to 18 minutes or until golden brown. Serve with remaining salsa. Makes 16 biscuits or 8 servings.

extra point ● *Substitute boneless skinless chicken breasts for the pork chops, if desired.*

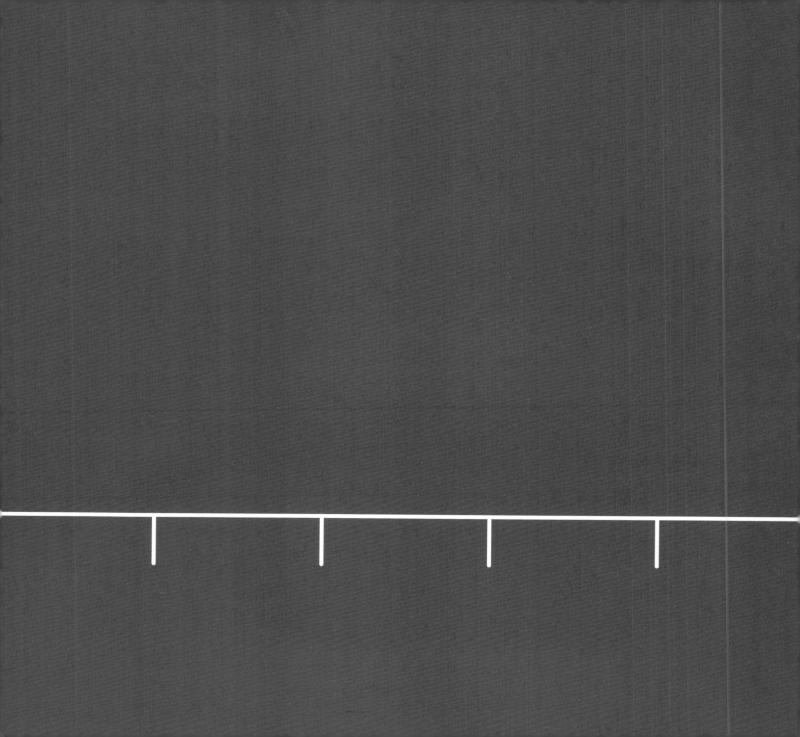

THE GRIDIRON

grilled to perfection

Football fields were originally called "gridirons" because they resembled a flat framework of parallel metal bars used for broiling meat. Isn't it funny that grilling meats just outside the football field would become so popular today?

Please see the helpful suggestions for successfully grilling meats on the following pages.

BEEF

- Beef burgers are the time-honored favorite meat to grill at tailgate parties; however, steaks are also a great choice.

- For burgers, be sure the ground beef is fresh. It should be pink without any unpleasant odors or dark spots.

- Grill burgers over medium heat to keep them flavorful and juicy.

- Resist the temptation to press down on the burgers with a spatula while they grill.

- Burgers are done when the internal temperature reaches 160°.

- Steaks are done when the internal temperature reaches 145° for medium-rare and 160° for medium.

PORK

- Bratwursts, smoked sausages, hot dogs and wieners are favorite pork choices served at tailgating events. These processed pork products take only a few minutes to cook.

- Fresh pork favorites such as ribs, tenderloins, loins and chops take longer to cook.

- Add extra flavor and tenderness by marinating fresh pork for 60 minutes or more.

- Add extra flavor with the use of seasonings rubbed onto pork prior to cooking.

- To keep pork from drying out, do not overcook it.

- Pork should be cooked/grilled until the internal temperature reaches 160°.

CHICKEN

- Boneless skinless chicken breast halves are ideal for tailgating. It's best to marinate chicken breasts before grilling. Cook only about 7 to 8 minutes per side over direct medium-high heat. To preserve its moistness and tenderness, do not overcook.

- Bone-in, skin-on chicken is great for grilling over medium-low heat. This allows slow, even cooking and minimized flare-ups.

- Leaving the skin on actually adds flavor and keeps moistness in. If you prefer to grill chicken without the skin, spray chicken lightly with cooking spray to keep it from sticking to the grill.

- Cook chicken until the juices run clear and the internal temperature reaches 170° for boneless breasts and 180° for all other pieces.

FISH

- For fish steaks or whole fish, such as salmon, cook for about 7 to 8 minutes per side on medium to medium-hot grill.

- Add extra flavor and tenderness by marinating fish for 30 minutes or more.

- Fish is done when it just begins to flake when tested with a fork. Scallops and shrimp will not flake, but they should look opaque when done.

- For ease at tailgating parties, wrap fish in a double layer of foil. Cut slits in the foil to allow the juices to drain so the fish doesn't poach in its own juices.

USDA Hotline
Have a meat or poultry food safety question?
Call toll-free 800-535-4555 (weekdays 10–4 ET).

TANGY HONEY-BARBECUE BEEF STEAKS

The balsamic vinegar and green onions in this sauce give it a tangy flavor.

4 to 6 beef steaks (ribeye or top sirloin), cut 1 to
   1¼ inches thick (6 to 8 oz. each)

Tangy Barbecue Sauce:

1 cup catsup

⅓ cup balsamic vinegar or cider vinegar

⅓ cup pure clover honey
   (Burleson's Honey recommended)

¼ cup thinly sliced green onions

¼ teaspoon salt

2 or 3 dashes bottled hot pepper sauce (or to taste)

Preheat grill to medium. Grill steaks over medium heat until desired doneness, turning once halfway through grilling. (Allow 8 to 12 minutes for medium-rare and 12 to 15 minutes for medium.) Meanwhile, in small saucepan, heat sauce ingredients to boiling. Reduce heat and simmer, uncovered, 10 to 15 minutes or until desired consistency, stirring often. Brush on steaks during last 3 minutes of grilling. Pass remaining sauce. Makes 4 to 6 servings.

extra point

Add the sauce during the last 3 to 5 minutes of grilling to keep the sauce from burning.

HERB-RUBBED PORK LOIN WITH HONEY-ONION BBQ SAUCE

The mellow sweet-sour flavor of this vinegar-based sauce will have you coming back for more.

1 boneless pork loin (2 to 2½ lb.)

Herb Rub:

2 teaspoons dried rosemary leaves, crushed

2 teaspoons dried thyme leaves, crushed

2 teaspoons ground cumin

1 teaspoon coarsely ground black pepper

1 teaspoon garlic salt

Honey-Onion BBQ Sauce:

2 tablespoons canola oil

1½ cups finely chopped onion

½ cup balsamic vinegar

½ cup pure clover honey

(Burleson's Honey recommended)

Combine Herb Rub ingredients; rub evenly onto pork. Preheat grill to medium-high. Grill pork over medium-high heat 15 minutes per side to brown slightly. Reduce heat to low (or place pork over indirect heat) and grill 35 to 45 minutes longer. Meanwhile, in small saucepan, heat oil over medium heat, swirling to coat pan. Add onion; cook and stir 5 minutes or until onion is translucent. Stir in vinegar and honey. Heat to boiling. Reduce heat and simmer, uncovered, 15 minutes, stirring occasionally. When internal temperature of pork reaches 160°, brush sauce on all sides of pork. Grill 10 minutes more. Pass remaining sauce. Makes 8 to 10 servings.

 extra point

Pork tenderloin can be used in place of pork loin in this recipe. Just reduce the grilling time to 30 minutes total.

HONEY-BARBECUE CHICKEN

This barbecue sauce is truly finger-lickin' good. A little lemon juice adds zip.

4 to 6 split chicken breast halves (bone-in)
Honey-Barbecue Sauce:
1 medium onion, finely chopped (1 cup)
¼ cup (½ stick) butter or margarine
1 cup catsup
⅓ cup water

¼ cup pure clover honey
   (Burleson's Honey recommended)
2 tablespoons lemon juice
1 tablespoon Worcestershire sauce
¼ teaspoon ground black pepper

Preheat grill to medium-high. Grill chicken over medium-high heat 10 minutes per side to brown slightly. Reduce heat to low (or place chicken over indirect heat) and grill 40 to 50 minutes longer or until internal temperature of chicken reaches 180°. Meanwhile, in small saucepan, cook and stir onion and butter over medium heat until onion is tender. Stir in remaining ingredients; heat to boiling. Reduce heat and simmer, uncovered, 5 minutes. Brush sauce on chicken during last 10 minutes of grilling. Pass remaining sauce. Makes 4 to 6 servings.

extra point

If you like your foods extra saucy, simply double the sauce recipe. Store leftover sauce in the refrigerator for up to 1 week.

HONEY-GINGER SALMON

Make this special heart-healthy entree for your football fans to enjoy.

1½ lb. salmon fillet, about 1 inch thick, cut
   into 6 pieces
Marinade:
½ cup orange juice
2 tablespoons chopped fresh cilantro
1 tablespoon canola oil

1 tablespoon peeled and minced fresh ginger
¼ teaspoon salt
¼ cup pure clover honey
   (Burleson's Honey recommended)

Place salmon in glass baking dish. In small bowl, stir together orange juice, cilantro, oil, ginger and salt. Pour over salmon and marinate for at least 30 minutes. Preheat broiler. Remove salmon to a broiler rack that has been placed in a baking pan and coated with cooking spray. Broil (about 5 inches from heat) about 5 minutes per side or until salmon is nearly opaque in the center. Meanwhile, add honey to orange juice marinade. Microwave mixture on High for 1 minute or until boiling. Pour over salmon and grill or broil 2 minutes longer or until salmon flakes easily with fork. Makes 6 servings.

Grilling Instructions: Preheat grill to medium-high. Place salmon directly on grill, skin-side down. Grill for about 7 minutes per side or until salmon begins to flake.

Purchase one large salmon fillet, then cut it into serving-size pieces prior to marinating. This marinade is great on boneless, skinless chicken breasts, too.

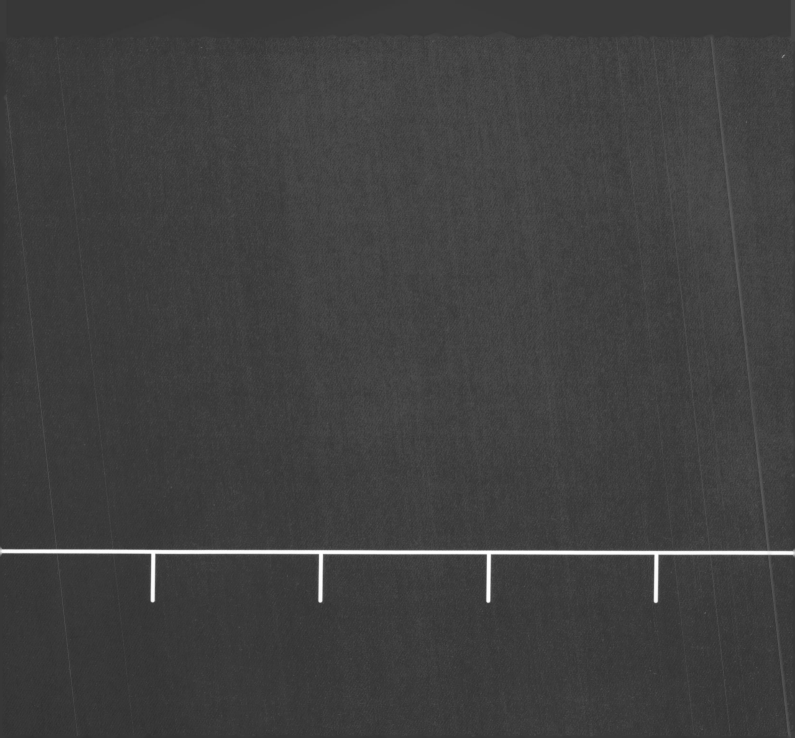

SIDELINES

sauces, salsas + spreads

When we think of football, we imagine fans everywhere gathered near the backs of their SUVs or in front of their televisions eating...drinking...and rooting for their favorite teams. Many football fanatics will work up hearty appetites just watching their favorite teams play. Make your game-watching gathering a tasty event with these "sidelines." Add sauces, salsas or spreads to your favorite burgers, brats and sausages.

BASIC HONEY BARBECUE SAUCE

1 medium onion, finely chopped (1 cup)
¼ cup (½ stick) butter or margarine
1 cup catsup
⅓ cup water
¼ cup pure clover honey
   (Burleson's Honey recommended)

2 tablespoons lemon juice
1 tablespoon Worcestershire sauce
¼ teaspoon ground black pepper

In small saucepan over medium-high heat, cook and stir onion and butter until onion is tender. Stir in remaining ingredients. Heat to boiling. Reduce heat and simmer, uncovered, 5 minutes to blend flavors. Brush on beef, chicken or pork during the last 10 minutes of grilling. If desired, reheat and pass remaining sauce. Makes 1½ cups sauce.

HONEY-BEER BARBECUE SAUCE

1 small onion, finely chopped (½ cup)
1 clove garlic, minced
1 tablespoon canola oil
1 cup chili sauce
½ cup beer

⅓ cup pure clover honey
   (Burleson's Honey recommended)
2 tablespoons Worcestershire sauce
4 teaspoons prepared mustard

In small saucepan over medium-high heat, cook and stir onion and garlic in oil until onion is tender. Stir in remaining ingredients. Heat to boiling. Reduce heat and simmer, uncovered, about 20 minutes or until desired consistency, stirring occasionally. Brush on beef, chicken or pork during the last 10 minutes of grilling. If desired, reheat and pass remaining sauce. Makes about 1½ cups sauce.

extra point   ● *These barbecue sauces are great served with beef, chicken or pork.*

SWEET AND SPICY CARIBBEAN BBQ SAUCE

1 medium onion, chopped (1 cup)
3 cloves garlic, minced
2 tablespoons canola or vegetable oil
½ cup chili sauce
¼ cup pure clover honey
   (Burleson's Honey recommended)

½ teaspoon salt
½ teaspoon ground allspice
½ teaspoon ground ginger
¼ teaspoon ground nutmeg

In small saucepan over medium-high heat, cook and stir onion and garlic in oil until onion is tender. Stir in remaining ingredients. Heat to boiling. Reduce heat and simmer, uncovered, 5 minutes to blend flavors. Brush on beef, chicken or pork during the last 10 minutes of grilling. If desired, reheat and pass remaining sauce. Makes about 1 cup sauce.

SOUTHERN-STYLE HONEY BBQ SAUCE

1 small onion, chopped (½ cup)
2 tablespoons butter or margarine
⅓ cup pure clover honey
   (Burleson's Honey recommended)
¼ cup cider vinegar

¼ cup lemon juice
2 teaspoons Worcestershire sauce
½ teaspoon salt
½ teaspoon coarsely ground black pepper
¼ teaspoon ground mustard (dry)

In small saucepan over medium-high heat, cook and stir onion and butter until onion is tender. Stir in remaining ingredients. Heat to boiling. Reduce heat and simmer, uncovered, about 15 minutes to blend flavors. Brush on beef, chicken or pork during the last 10 minutes of grilling. If desired, reheat and pass remaining sauce. Makes about 1 cup sauce.

 extra point ● *These barbecue sauces can be made 1 week in advance.*

AVOCADO SALSA

1 large tomato, seeded and chopped (1 cup)

1 ripe avocado, peeled and chopped

2 tablespoons sliced green onions

2 tablespoons fresh lime juice (about ½ lime)

1 tablespoon chopped fresh cilantro

1 tablespoon vegetable oil

¼ teaspoon salt

In medium bowl, combine all ingredients. Serve over grilled burgers, chicken or salmon. Makes about 1½ cups salsa.

ROASTED RED PEPPER SALSA

1 jar (7 oz.) roasted red peppers, drained and chopped (about 1 cup)

¼ cup sliced green onions

1 tablespoon chopped fresh cilantro

¼ teaspoon salt

In medium bowl, combine all ingredients. Serve over grilled burgers or steaks. Makes about 1½ cups salsa.

BLACK BEAN SALSA

1 can (15 oz.) black beans, rinsed and drained

1 medium cucumber, peeled, seeded and chopped

1 medium tomato, seeded and chopped

½ cup sliced green onions

¼ cup fresh lime juice (about 1 lime)

1 tablespoon chopped fresh cilantro

1 tablespoon olive oil

½ teaspoon salt

½ teaspoon ground cumin

⅛ teaspoon ground red pepper

In medium bowl, combine all ingredients. Cover and refrigerate for several hours to blend flavors. Serve over grilled pork, smoked bratwursts or sausages, grilled chicken or salmon. Makes about 2 cups salsa.

extra point

● *Cilantro, also called Chinese parsley or coriander, is sold in bunches in the produce section.*

CREAMY DIJON MUSTARD SAUCE

½ cup real mayonnaise

½ cup sour cream

4 teaspoons Dijon-style mustard

3 tablespoons finely chopped green onion

Stir together all ingredients. Serve with grilled burgers. Makes about 1 cup sauce.

EASY CREAMY ITALIAN HERB SPREAD

1 package (3 oz.) cream cheese, softened

¼ cup (½ stick) butter or margarine, softened

1 clove garlic, minced

1 teaspoon dried Italian seasoning

⅛ teaspoon ground white pepper

Process all ingredients in food processor or blender until smooth. Serve with grilled burgers. Makes about ¾ cup spread.

BLUE CHEESE SPREAD

½ cup (1 stick) butter or margarine, softened

¼ cup crumbled blue cheese

2 tablespoons grated Parmesan cheese

In mixer bowl, beat ingredients until almost smooth. Serve with grilled burgers. Makes about ¾ cup spread.

SOUTHWESTERN SPREAD

1 package (3 oz.) cream cheese, softened

⅓ cup butter or margarine, softened

1 tablespoon chopped fresh cilantro

1 clove garlic, minced

2 drops hot pepper sauce

Process all ingredients in food processor or blender until smooth. Serve with grilled burgers. Makes about ¾ cup spread.

 extra point ◗ *These spreads are great served on grilled beef, pork or turkey burgers.*

SUPER BOWLS

chilis, soups + stews

Few days in the lives of sports fans everywhere are as celebrated as Super Bowl Sunday. And since most of us only watch the game from afar—via the television—it has also become a major food fiesta.

When it comes to the perfect game day fare, here are some great recipes that are sure to please football fanatics everywhere. Choose recipes that are super easy so you can have everything ready ahead of time—meaning you get to enjoy the game, too.

BOWL GAME CHILI

This hearty low-fat chili features flavors from the Southwest.

1 lb. lean ground beef
1 large onion, chopped (2 cups)
3½ cups water (divided)
2 cans (14½ oz. each) diced Mexican-style or
   chili-style tomatoes
2 cans (15 oz. each) black beans or pinto beans,
   rinsed and drained

2 cups picante sauce
1 teaspoon ground cumin (optional)
1 package (1.61 oz.) brown gravy mix
   (Pioneer Brand recommended)
Shredded Cheddar cheese

In 4-quart saucepan or Dutch oven, cook and stir ground beef and onion until beef is no longer pink; drain. Add 3 cups water, tomatoes, beans, picante sauce and cumin; heat to boiling. Meanwhile, dissolve gravy mix in ½ cup cool water; stir into boiling soup. Reduce heat and simmer 10 minutes. Top with cheese and serve with Chili Cheese Herb Biscuits (below). Makes 8 to 10 servings.

CHILI CHEESE HERB BISCUITS

These savory biscuits are sure to become a family favorite.

3 cups buttermilk biscuit & baking mix
   (Pioneer Brand recommended)
1 cup finely shredded Colby, Monterey Jack or
   Cheddar cheese
1 cup milk

1 can (4 oz.) chopped green chilies, drained well
6 tablespoons (¾ stick) butter or margarine,
   melted
1 tablespoon dried parsley flakes
½ teaspoon garlic powder

In large bowl, stir together biscuit and baking mix, cheese, milk and chilies until moistened. Drop dough by spoonfuls onto baking sheet coated with cooking spray. Bake at 450° for 10 to 13 minutes or until biscuits are golden brown. Combine butter, parsley and garlic powder; brush on biscuits. Serve warm. Makes 16 to 18 biscuits.

extra point

● *For variety, use 1 can each of black beans and pinto beans in the chili.*

CHICKEN CHILI

White beans, green chilies and cumin give this chili an authentic Tex–Mex flavor.

1 lb. boneless skinless chicken breasts, cut into
  ½-inch pieces
1 large onion, chopped (2 cups)
1 tablespoon vegetable oil
2 cans (15 oz. each) great northern beans or
  garbanzo beans, rinsed and drained
2 cans (14½ oz. each) chicken broth

1 can (4 oz.) chopped green chilies
2 teaspoons ground cumin
1 package (2.75 oz.) country gravy mix
  (Pioneer Brand recommended)
1 cup cool water
Hot pepper sauce (optional)

In 4-quart saucepan or Dutch oven, cook and stir chicken and onion in oil over medium-high heat for 5 to 7 minutes, until onion is tender. Add beans, chicken broth, green chilies and cumin; heat to boiling. Meanwhile, dissolve gravy mix in water. Stir into boiling mixture until thickened. Reduce heat; cover and simmer for 15 to 20 minutes to allow flavors to blend. Add hot pepper sauce to taste. Garnish with fresh cilantro sprigs. Serve with Roasted Red Pepper Drop Biscuits (below). Makes 6 servings.

ROASTED RED PEPPER DROP BISCUITS

Make these melt–in–your–mouth biscuits to complement any hearty soup.

2 cups buttermilk biscuit & baking mix
  (Pioneer Brand recommended)
1 cup sour cream

¼ cup (½ stick) butter or margarine, melted
2 tablespoons drained and finely chopped roasted
  red peppers

In medium bowl, stir together all ingredients until well combined. Drop dough by spoonfuls onto baking sheet coated with cooking spray. Bake at 400° for 12 to 16 minutes or until biscuits are golden brown. Serve warm. Makes 12 to 14 biscuits.

extra point

Look for roasted red bell peppers next to condiments and pickles at the supermarket.

MEXICAN MEATBALL AND SALSA CHILI

When you want something extra "meaty," make this meat-lover's chili!

1½ lb. lean ground beef
½ cup dry bread crumbs
½ teaspoon salt
¼ teaspoon pepper
1 medium onion, chopped (1 cup)
2 teaspoons vegetable oil
2½ cups water (divided)

2 cans (14½ oz. each) diced Mexican-style or
  chili-style tomatoes
2 cups salsa (mild, medium or hot)
2 teaspoons ground cumin
1 teaspoon chili powder
1 teaspoon finely chopped jalapeño pepper (opt.)
1 package (1.61 oz.) brown gravy mix
  (Pioneer Brand recommended)

In large bowl, stir together ground beef, bread crumbs, salt and pepper; shape into 1-inch balls. Place on rimmed baking sheet. Bake at 400° for 15 minutes or until meatballs are no longer pink inside. Meanwhile, in 4-quart saucepan or Dutch oven, cook and stir onion in oil until tender. Add 2 cups water, tomatoes, salsa, cumin, chili powder and jalapeño pepper; heat to boiling. Dissolve gravy mix in ½ cup cool water; stir into boiling mixture. Add meatballs; reduce heat and simmer 10 minutes to combine flavors. Makes 8 servings.

CHEESY RANCH PINWHEELS

Ranch salad dressing adds a zesty flavor to these pretty pinwheels.

3 cups buttermilk biscuit & baking mix
  (Pioneer Brand recommended)
1 tablespoon chopped fresh cilantro

1 cup milk
3 tablespoons prepared ranch salad dressing
1 cup finely shredded Colby-Jack cheese

In large bowl, stir together biscuit and baking mix, cilantro and milk to form a stiff dough. Turn out onto surface dusted with additional biscuit and baking mix; knead 10 times. Roll out dough into rectangle about ½-inch thick. Spread with salad dressing; sprinkle with cheese. Beginning with long side, roll up like a jelly roll. Cut into 12 to 14 slices (½ to ¾-inch thick); place slices on baking sheet coated with cooking spray. Bake at 400° for 10 to 12 minutes or until pinwheels are golden brown. Serve warm. Makes 12 to 14 pinwheels.

extra point

● *Use unflavored dental floss to "cut" through the biscuit dough to make even slices.*

BLACK AND WHITE "REFEREE" CHILI

This hearty soup combines white chicken breast with black beans—in honor of the referees.

1 large onion, chopped (2 cups)

1 cup chopped celery

1 tablespoon vegetable oil

1 to 1½ lb. boneless skinless chicken breasts,
 cut into ½-inch pieces

2 cans (14½ oz. each) or 1 carton (32 oz.)
 chicken broth

1 can (4 oz.) chopped green chilies

2 teaspoons ground cumin

1 package (2.75 oz.) country gravy mix
 (Pioneer Brand recommended)

½ cup cool water

2 cans (15 oz. each) black beans, rinsed and drained

¼ cup chopped fresh cilantro

In 4-quart saucepan or Dutch oven, cook and stir onion and celery in oil over medium-high heat for 5 to 7 minutes, until onion is tender. Add chicken and cook until chicken is no longer pink. Add chicken broth, green chilies and cumin; heat to boiling. Meanwhile, dissolve gravy mix in water. Stir into boiling soup; cook and stir until thickened. Cover and simmer for 10 minutes to allow flavors to blend. Stir in beans and cilantro; heat through. Serve with Peppered Sour Cream Biscuits (below). Makes 8 servings.

PEPPERED SOUR CREAM BISCUITS

The contrast in flavors is just as pleasing as the contrast in colors.

3 cups low-protein self-rising flour
 (White Lily Brand recommended)

¼ teaspoon garlic-seasoned black pepper

1 cup sour cream

⅔ cup milk

¼ cup (½ stick) butter or margarine, melted

In large bowl, stir together all ingredients to form a ball. Turn out onto surface dusted with additional flour; knead dough by folding it in half 5 to 7 times. Roll out or pat dough to ½-inch thickness. With biscuit cutter, cut into 3-inch rounds. Place on baking sheet coated with cooking spray. Brush with additional melted butter, if desired. Bake at 450° for 13 to 15 minutes or until biscuits are golden brown. Serve warm. Makes 12 biscuits.

extra point

❧ *Chilies, ground cumin and country gravy mix add just the right flavor and thickness to this soup.*

EASY CHICKEN AND DUMPLINGS

This updated version of a homey classic is so quick and easy, you'll want to make it frequently.

Dumplings:
1½ cups low-protein self-rising flour
   (White Lily Brand recommended)
1 tablespoon chopped fresh parsley (or
   1 teaspoon dried parsley flakes)
3 tablespoons butter or margarine, melted
2 tablespoons milk or buttermilk
1 large egg, beaten
Soup:
1 medium onion, chopped (1 cup)

1 cup chopped celery
2 tablespoons olive oil or vegetable oil
1½ lb. boneless skinless chicken breasts, cut into
   ½-inch pieces
2 cans (14½ oz. each) or 1 carton (32 oz.)
   chicken broth
2 cups water
½ teaspoon coarsely ground black pepper
¼ teaspoon salt
1 cup thinly sliced carrots

In medium bowl, stir together flour, parsley, butter, milk and egg until dough forms. Turn out onto surface dusted with additional flour; knead 5 times. Roll out dough to ¼-inch thickness. Cut into 2-inch-wide strips, then into 2-inch pieces; set aside. In 4-quart saucepan or Dutch oven, cook and stir onion and celery in oil over medium-high heat for 5 minutes. Add chicken; cook and stir for 3 to 5 minutes or until chicken is no longer pink inside. Add broth, water, pepper and salt; heat to boiling. Cover; reduce heat and simmer 5 minutes. Increase heat to bring soup to full rolling boil; add carrots. Add dumplings one at a time. Cover and simmer, stirring occasionally, for 10 minutes or until dumplings are cooked and carrots are tender. Makes 8 servings.

extra point

🖤 *Fresh parsley makes these dumplings especially flavorful and attractive.*

TEX-MEX CHEESY CHICKEN CHOWDER

The zesty Mexican flavors in this chowder will satisfy any football fan.

1 medium onion, chopped (1 cup)

1 cup thinly sliced celery

2 cloves garlic, minced

1 tablespoon vegetable oil

1½ lb. boneless skinless chicken breasts, cut into
  ½-inch pieces

2 cans (14½ oz. each) chicken broth

1 bag (32 oz.) frozen hash-brown potatoes, thawed

1 package (2.75 oz.) country gravy mix
  (Pioneer Brand recommended)

2 cups milk

8 oz. pasteurized prepared cheese product, cubed
  (Velveeta recommended)

2 cups chunky salsa

1 can (4 oz.) chopped green chilies

In 4-quart saucepan or Dutch oven, cook and stir onion, celery and garlic in oil over medium heat for 5 minutes, or until onion is tender. Add chicken; cook and stir until chicken is no longer pink inside. Add chicken broth; heat to boiling. Add potatoes; cover and simmer for 10 to 15 minutes or until potatoes are cooked, stirring occasionally. Return to boiling. Meanwhile, dissolve gravy mix in milk; stir into boiling soup. Add cheese, salsa and green chilies. Cook and stir over low heat until cheese is melted. Makes 8 servings.

HOT AND BUTTERY BISCUIT SQUARES

So easy to make! So delicious to eat!

3 cups buttermilk biscuit & baking mix
  (Pioneer Brand recommended)

1 cup sour cream

½ cup milk

3 tablespoons butter or margarine, melted

Measure baking mix into large bowl. In small bowl, stir together sour cream and milk; stir into baking mix to form a soft dough. Turn out onto surface dusted with additional baking mix; knead 10 times. Place in an 8x8-inch baking pan coated with cooking spray. Press to fit pan. Cut into 16 squares. Brush top with butter. Bake at 400° for 15 to 18 minutes or until biscuits are golden brown. Serve warm or at room temperature. Makes 16 biscuits.

extra point

● *Keep it simple! Convenience foods such as canned chicken broth, frozen hash browns, gravy mix and prepared salsa make this soup a cinch to prepare.*

HALF-TIME SHOW

main entrees

Many of us will never attend a Super Bowl game. Rather, we'll gather around our TVs to watch the biggest, most important football game of the year from the comfort of our homes. While we may not experience the sheer excitement of being at the game, we can certainly enjoy tastier and more satisfying food than the vendors offer.

   Stay home and enjoy the comforts of eating in your family room as you relax and watch the game.

FABULOUS FIESTA FOOTBALL FOOD

Everyone will love this meal—in—a—dish, with its taco seasonings and whole kernel corn.

Pastry:
⅓ cup firm butter or margarine
⅓ cup shortening
2 cups low-protein all-purpose flour
   (White Lily Brand recommended)
1 teaspoon salt
⅓ cup plus 1 tablespoon cold water
Filling:
1½ lb. extra-lean ground beef
1 package (1¼ oz.) taco seasoning mix
½ cup water

1 package (1.61 oz.) brown gravy mix
   (Pioneer Brand recommended)
1½ cups milk
1 can (11 or 15 oz.) whole kernel corn with red
   and green bell peppers, drained
1 can (15 oz.) black beans, rinsed and drained
1 cup shredded Cheddar cheese
Cilantro Sauce:
1 cup sour cream
2 tablespoons chopped fresh cilantro

For Pastry, in medium bowl, using a pastry blender or two knives, cut butter and shortening into flour and salt until mixture is crumbly. Gently stir in water just until dough holds together in a ball. Wrap tightly in plastic wrap and chill until ready to use. *For Filling*, in large skillet, cook and stir beef, taco seasoning mix and water over medium heat for 5 minutes. In 2-cup glass measure, stir together gravy mix and milk; add to cooked beef mixture. Cook and stir until thickened. Pour into 13x9x2-inch or 2-quart totable baking dish coated with cooking spray. Layer corn, black beans and cheese over beef mixture. Set aside. On surface dusted with additional flour, roll out pastry dough to ⅛-inch thickness. Use a football-shaped cookie cutter to cut out pastry shapes and place them on a baking sheet coated with cooking spray. Bake both the casserole and the pastry at 425° for 10 to 20 minutes or until pastry is golden brown and casserole is heated through. Meanwhile, stir together sour cream and cilantro. When ready to serve, place the baked pastry footballs over the casserole. Spoon a dollop of the Cilantro Sauce over each serving. Garnish with chopped red bell pepper, if desired. Makes 8 servings.

Alternately, cut pastry into 1—inch—wide strips. Place unbaked strips over casserole, crisscrossing them to cover. Bake 25 to 28 minutes.

MEAT-N-POTATOES-N-GRAVY MEAT LOAF

This appetite-pleasin' all-in-one meal is perfect game-time fare.

Meat Loaf:
2 large eggs
½ cup catsup
⅓ cup water
2 tablespoons Worcestershire sauce
1 cup dry bread crumbs
¾ cup finely chopped onion
1 package (1.61 oz.) brown gravy mix
   (Pioneer Brand recommended)
1½ lb. lean ground beef

2½ cups frozen southern-style hash-brown
   potatoes, thawed slightly
Gravy:
1 package (1.61 oz.) brown gravy mix
   (Pioneer Brand recommended)
1½ cups cool water (divided)
⅔ cup catsup
¼ cup packed brown sugar
2 tablespoons prepared mustard

In large bowl, stir together all meat loaf ingredients except ground beef and potatoes. Add beef and potatoes; mix well. Pat mixture into 9x5x3-inch loaf pan coated with cooking spray. Bake at 350° for 50 minutes. Meanwhile, dissolve 1 package gravy mix in ½ cup cool water; set aside. In 2-cup glass measure, microwave 1 cup water on high for 3 minutes or until boiling. Stir in dissolved gravy; microwave on High for 1 minute or until thickened. Stir in catsup, brown sugar and mustard. Pour ¾ cup gravy mixture over baked meat loaf. Bake 20 minutes more. Microwave remaining gravy mixture until hot. Serve with meat loaf. Makes 8 servings.

extra point

● *This easy-to-tackle meat loaf has everything combined into one—lean ground beef, southern-style hash-brown potatoes and savory brown gravy.*

KICK-OFF BRISKET

Bloody Mary mix provides a real taste "kick" in this saucy beef brisket.

1 large onion, sliced
1 extra-lean beef brisket (4½ to 5 lb.), all
   visible fat removed
1 cup Bloody Mary mix (mild or hot)
1 cup lemon-lime soda (8 oz.)

Juice of 1 lemon (about ⅓ cup)
2 teaspoons Worcestershire sauce
1 package (1.61 oz.) brown gravy mix
   (Pioneer Brand recommended)

Layer onions and beef in large roaster or 13x9x2-inch baking pan or dish. In 4-cup glass measure, stir together Bloody Mary mix, lemon-lime soda, lemon juice and Worcestershire sauce; whisk in gravy mix. Pour over beef; cover tightly with foil. Bake at 325° for 3 hours or until beef is tender when pierced with a fork. Cool for 15 to 20 minutes. Cut across the grain into thin slices. Arrange beef in 13x9x2-inch baking dish or totable carrier. Pour sauce over beef. Cover; keep warm until serving time or refrigerate and reheat as needed. Serve with "Game Thyme" Biscuit Squares (below). Makes 8 to 10 servings.

"GAME THYME" BISCUIT SQUARES

Sour cream makes these easy biscuits extra moist.

3 cups buttermilk biscuit & baking mix
   (Pioneer Brand recommended)
1 tablespoon finely chopped fresh parsley
½ teaspoon dried thyme leaves

1 cup sour cream
½ cup milk
2 tablespoons butter or margarine, melted

In large bowl, stir together baking mix, parsley and thyme. In 2-cup glass measure, combine sour cream and milk; stir into baking mix mixture until dough forms a ball. Turn out onto surface dusted with additional baking mix. Knead 10 times. Place in 8x6x3-inch totable dish. Using a knife, cut dough into squares. Drizzle with butter. Bake at 400° for 18 to 20 minutes or until golden brown. Cover loosely; keep warm until serving or reheat as needed. Makes 12 biscuits.

extra point

● *When baking the brisket, cover the baking pan tightly with foil to allow the steam to help tenderize the beef.*

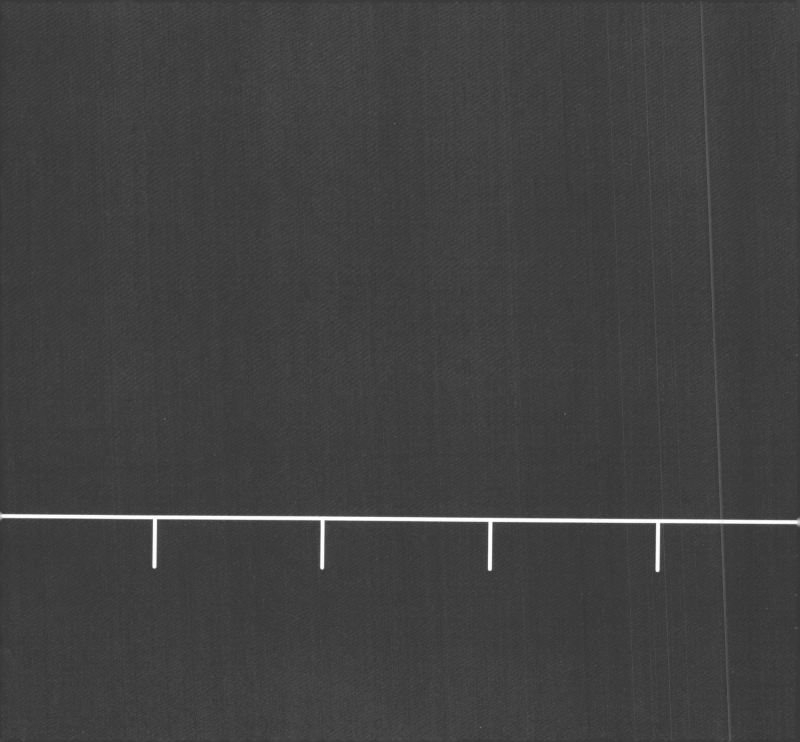

TOUCHDOWNS!

sweet victories

Impress your friends and family with sweet treats during and after the game. Some of the recipes on the following pages can be shaped and decorated to resemble footballs. They're so easy to make, you'll be ready to celebrate your team's victory before you know it! Your family and friends will surely be "huddling" around the plate for more.

You can find football-shaped cookie cutters in many supermarkets during the fall months, as well as in kitchen and cookware stores throughout the year.

FOOTBALL BISCUITS WITH CARAMEL-APPLE FONDUE

Indulge yourself with these rich but light—as—a—feather biscuits dipped in caramel apple fondue.

Football Biscuits:
2½ cups low-protein self-rising flour
   (White Lily Brand recommended)
2 tablespoons sugar
1½ cups heavy (whipping) cream
2 tablespoons butter or margarine, melted

Caramel-Apple Fondue:
1 carton (16 oz.) prepared caramel apple dip
   (2 cups)
2 Golden Delicious or Granny Smith apples,
   peeled, cored and finely chopped
½ cup toasted finely chopped pecans (optional)
2 tablespoons butter or margarine, softened

In large bowl, stir together flour, sugar and cream until dough forms a ball. Turn out onto surface dusted with additional flour. Fold dough in half about 3 to 5 times to knead (do not overwork dough), adding just enough flour to keep dough from sticking to your hands. Roll out dough to ½-inch thickness. Using a 1½-inch football-shaped cookie cutter coated with flour, cut dough into biscuits. Re-roll and cut remaining dough as needed. Place biscuits about 1 inch apart on baking sheet coated with cooking spray. Using a sharp knife, make cuts in top of each "football" to resemble laces, being careful not to cut all the way through dough. Brush with melted butter. Bake at 450° for 10 minutes or until biscuits are golden brown. Meanwhile, stir together caramel dip, apple, nuts and 2 tablespoons butter. Microwave on High for 1 minute, stirring every 30 seconds, until caramel is melted and heated through. Transfer to fondue server or warming server. Serve with Football Biscuits. Makes 20 to 24 biscuits or 10 to 12 servings.

extra point

Dip the cutter into the flour before cutting each biscuit. For evenly shaped biscuits with straight sides, press the cutter straight down without twisting.

SWEET AND SPICY FOOTBALL COOKIES

Your guests won't fumble when you pass them these football-shaped cookies!

1 cup packed dark brown sugar

1 cup (2 sticks) butter or margarine, softened

1 large egg

1 teaspoon ground ginger

½ teaspoon ground cinnamon

⅛ teaspoon ground cloves

2¾ cups buttermilk biscuit & baking mix
(Pioneer Brand recommended)

1 cup white "chocolate" chips (6 oz.)

2 teaspoons shortening

In large mixer bowl, beat brown sugar and butter until creamy, about 3 minutes. Add egg, ginger, cinnamon and cloves; beat until light and fluffy. Add biscuit and baking mix, beating on low speed to combine. Chill dough for at least 1 hour. On surface dusted with additional biscuit and baking mix, roll out half of dough to ⅛-inch thickness. With cookie cutter, cut out football shapes (or other shapes as desired). Place 1 inch apart on cookie sheets coated with cooking spray. Bake at 350° for 10 to 12 minutes or until tops are no longer moist. Remove from cookie sheet to wire rack to cool. Repeat with remaining dough. To decorate, place white chocolate chips and shortening in heavy-duty resealable plastic bag; microwave on Medium (50% power) for 3 to 4 minutes, massaging bag every minute, or until chips are melted. Cut off tip of one corner of bag. Pipe melted white chocolate onto cookies to resemble laces on footballs. Makes 4 to 5 dozen cookies, depending on size of cutter.

extra point

● *To make sandwich cookies, spread additional melted white chocolate on top of cookie. Top with another cookie. Decorate as directed above.*

TOUCHDOWN TURNOVERS

A chocolate football is tucked inside each of these tasty turnovers—surprise!

2 cups buttermilk biscuit & baking mix
  (Pioneer Brand recommended)
1¼ cups flaked coconut (divided)
⅔ cup milk
⅓ cup sweetened condensed milk
  (¼ of a 14-oz. can)

15 milk chocolate football candies, unwrapped
  (Hershey's Brand recommended)
2 tablespoons butter or margarine, melted
⅓ cup milk chocolate chips
1 teaspoon shortening

In large bowl, stir together biscuit and baking mix, ½ cup of the coconut and milk to form soft dough. Turn out onto surface dusted with additional biscuit and baking mix; knead 10 to 15 times. Roll out dough to a 15x9-inch rectangle. Cut into 15 (3x3-inch) squares. Place squares on baking sheet coated with cooking spray. Combine remaining coconut and sweetened condensed milk. Spoon 1 rounded teaspoonful of coconut mixture onto center of each square; top with chocolate football. Fold dough in half to form a triangle. Press edges together with fork to seal. Brush turnovers with melted butter. Bake at 400° for 10 to 13 minutes or until golden brown. Meanwhile, place ⅓ cup chocolate chips and shortening in heavy-duty resealable plastic bag. Microwave on Medium (50% power) for 2 to 3 minutes or until chips are melted, massaging bag every minute. Cut off tip of one corner of bag. Drizzle melted chocolate over turnovers. Makes 15 turnovers.

extra point

● *When measuring biscuit and baking mix, gently spoon mix into nested (dry) measuring cup/s. Level off the top using a metal spatula.*

BANANA-NUT SANDWICH COOKIES

The banana–nut flavor of these cookies will have your friends scrambling for more!

Cookies:
1 package (8.1 oz.) banana nut muffin mix
  (White Lily Brand recommended)
¾ cup low-protein all-purpose flour
  (White Lily Brand recommended)
¼ cup packed dark brown sugar
½ cup (1 stick) butter or margarine, melted and
  cooled slightly

Butter Cream Filling:
1½ cups sifted powdered sugar
½ cup (1 stick) butter or margarine, softened
1 teaspoon vanilla
Decoration:
½ cup white or semisweet chocolate chips
2 teaspoons shortening

In medium bowl, stir together muffin mix, flour, brown sugar and ½ cup butter until dough forms. On surface dusted with additional flour, roll out dough to ⅛- to ¼-inch thickness. Using a football-shaped cookie cutter, cut out cookies. Place on cookie sheet coated with cooking spray. Bake at 350° for 10 to 12 minutes or until cookies begin to brown. Remove cookies to wire rack to cook completely. Stir together filling ingredients until smooth. Spread filling on bottom of one cookie; put together with another cookie to make a cookie "sandwich." Repeat with remaining cookies and filling. Place chocolate chips and shortening in heavy-duty resealable plastic bag. Microwave on Medium (50% power) for 1 to 1½ minutes or until chips are melted and smooth, massaging bag every 30 seconds. Cut off tip of one corner of bag. Pipe melted chocolate onto cookies to resemble laces on footballs. Makes about 3½ dozen sandwich cookies.

extra point

● *For a different flavor sensation, substitute creamy peanut butter for the butter cream filling.*

END ZONE

A

Appetizers
Cheesy Pigs in Blankets, 23
Game Day Hearty Mexican Dip, 19
Pre-Game Pinwheels, 20
Tailgater's Tex-Mex Chili Dip, 16

B

Barbecue
Basic Honey Barbecue Sauce, 40
grilling tips, 28
Herb-Rubbed Pork Loin with Honey-Onion
 BBQ Sauce, 33
Honey-Barbecue Chicken, 34
Honey-Beer Barbecue Sauce, 40
Southern-Style Honey BBQ Sauce, 41
Sweet and Spicy Caribbean BBQ Sauce, 41
Tangy Barbecue Sauce, 30

Beans
Black and White "Referee" Chili, 53
Bowl Game Chili, 46
Chicken Chili, 49

Fabulous Fiesta Football Food, 60
Tailgater's Tex-Mex Chili Dip, 16

Beef
Bowl Game Chili, 46
Fabulous Fiesta Football Food, 60
Game Day Hearty Mexican Dip, 19
grilling tips, 28
Kick-Off Brisket, 64
Meat-n-Potatoes-n-Gravy Meat Loaf, 63
Mexican Meatball and Salsa Chili, 50
Tailgater's Tex-Mex Chili Dip, 16
Tangy Honey-Barbecue Beef Steaks, 30

Biscuits
Cheesy Pigs in Blankets, 23
Cheesy Ranch Pinwheels, 50
Chili Cheese Herb Biscuits, 46
Football Biscuits with Caramel-Apple
 Fondue, 68
Football Pork Pockets, 24
"Game Thyme" Biscuit Squares, 64
Hot and Buttery Biscuit Squares, 57
Peppered Sour Cream Biscuits, 53

Pre-Game Pinwheels, 20
Roasted Red Pepper Drop Biscuits, 49

C

Chicken
Black and White "Referee" Chili, 53
Chicken Chili, 49
Easy Chicken and Dumplings, 54
grilling tips, 29
Honey-Barbecue Chicken, 34
Tex-Mex Cheesy Chicken Chowder, 57

Chili. See Soups and stews
Cookies. See Desserts

D

Desserts
Banana-Nut Sandwich Cookies, 75
Football Biscuits with Caramel-Apple
 Fondue, 68
Sweet and Spicy Football Cookies, 71
Touchdown Turnovers, 72

Dips. See Appetizers

E

Entrees
  Fabulous Fiesta Football Food, 60
  Kick-Off Brisket with "Game Thyme"
   Biscuit Squares, 64
  Meat-n-Potatoes-n-Gravy Meat Loaf, 63

F

Fish
  grilling tips, 29
  Honey-Ginger Salmon, 37

H

Honey
  Basic Honey Barbecue Sauce, 40
  Herb-Rubbed Pork Loin with Honey-Onion
   BBQ Sauce, 33
  Honey-Barbecue Chicken, 34
  Honey-Beer Barbecue Sauce, 40
  Honey-Ginger Salmon, 37
  Honey-Onion Barbecue Sauce, 33
  Southern-Style Honey BBQ Sauce, 41
  Tangy Honey-Barbecue Beef Steaks, 30

M

Mexican
  Game Day Hearty Mexican Dip, 19
  Mexican Meatball and Salsa Chili, 50
  Tailgater's Tex-Mex Chili Dip, 16
  Tex-Mex Cheesy Chicken Chowder, 57

P

Pork
  Cheesy Pigs in Blankets, 23
  Football Pork Pockets, 24
  grilling tips, 28
  Herb-Rubbed Pork Loin with Honey-Onion
   BBQ Sauce, 33
  Tailgater's Tex-Mex Chili Dip, 16

Q

Quesadillas, Chili Dip, 16

S

Salsa
  Avocado Salsa, 42
  Black Bean Salsa, 42

  Football Pork Pockets, 24
  Mexican Meatball and Salsa Chili, 50
  Roasted Red Pepper Salsa, 42
  Tailgater's Tex-Mex Chili Dip, 16

Sauces
  Basic Honey Barbecue Sauce, 40
  Creamy Dijon Mustard Sauce, 43
  Honey-Beer Barbecue Sauce, 40
  Southern-Style Honey BBQ Sauce, 41
  Sweet and Spicy Caribbean BBQ Sauce, 41

Soups and stews
  Black and White "Referee" Chili, 53
  Bowl Game Chili, 46
  Chicken Chili, 49
  Easy Chicken and Dumplings, 54
  Mexican Meatball and Salsa Chili, 50
  Tex-Mex Cheesy Chicken Chowder, 57

Spreads
  Blue Cheese Spread, 43
  Easy Creamy Italian Herb Spread, 43
  Southwestern Spread, 43

U

USDA hotline, 29

COOKBOOK ORDER FORM

Tailgates to Touchdowns

If you know other football fanatics who would enjoy these recipes, just tell us where to ship the books.

I would like _____ additional copies of Tailgates to Touchdowns at $18.95 (Iowa residents must add sales tax, for a total of $19.90) plus $3.00 shipping and handling. Please ship to the following address. (If ordering more than one book, please indicate the address for each shipment desired.)

Name: _____

Address: _____

City: _____State: _____Zip: _____

Name: _____

Address: _____

City: _____State: _____Zip: _____

Make check payable to: Tailgates to Touchdowns

Mail check and order form to: Tailgates to Touchdowns Cookbook
PO Box 11151
Cedar Rapids, IA 52410

For more information, contact us at our Web site: **www.tailgatestotouchdowns.com**

If you can't find one of the products recommended in this cookbook, please visit the companies' Web sites for information on how to order their products.

www.pioneerbrand.com   www.whitelily.com   www.burlesons-honey.com